THE MAKING OF LEGACY AFRICA FILM

A medical doctor's struggles to produce a Hollywood-style movie.

THE MAKING OF LEGACY AFRICA FILM

A medical doctor's struggles to
produce a Hollywood-style movie.

R. Peprah-Gyamfi

Perseverance Books

THE MAKING OF LEGACY AFRICA FILM:
A medical doctor's struggles to produce a Hollywood-style movie.

Published by Perseverance Books, an imprint of
GLOBAL VILLAGE PUBLISHERS LTD

www.peprah-gyamfi.com
email: **info@peprah-gyamfi.com**

ISBN: 978-1-913285-40-1

www.peprah-gyamfi.com

Table of Contents

Chapter 1

Medical Doctor Turned Film Producer Cum Actor

There is a saying that one should "never say never". Another saying has it that "No one knows tomorrow."

Both sayings are relevant to the personal experience I am about to narrate. Indeed, never in my wildest dreams could I have foreseen that I would one day be producing a film , and not only produce a film, but also play the role of the lead actor.

How, then, did a medical doctor on the verge of retirement end up not only as a producer but also as the lead actor of a film?

To answer that question, I want to take the reader to my roots—the little village of Mpintmipi, located about 120 kilometres northwest of Ghana's capital, Accra.

Growing up in the little village, I experienced and also witnessed suffering all around me—too numerous to recount here.

I only want to cite three examples:

One day, as we walked home from school, we came across four people carrying someone on a makeshift stretcher. They emerged from a bush path that connected some nearby farmlands to the main road. We learned that the man they were carrying had been bitten by a snake while working on his farm, which was about one kilometre away. They tied a rope above the bite site on his left leg to help prevent the spread of the venom. Then, they carried him to the main road, hoping to find a vehicle that could take him to the hospital in Nkawkaw, which is about thirty kilometers north of our village.

Knowing that vehicles only sporadically travelled that road, I couldn't help but wonder if they would ever reach the hospital in time.

Next was the case of Dugiri, a young girl from the village, one of my playmates, aged about ten years. She sustained a deep cut wound to her right thigh whilst handling a machete. As blood oozed profusely from her vessels, the alarmed villagers instinctively tied a cord firmly above the wound in a desperate attempt to stop or at least minimize the loss of blood. We waited for a vehicle to pass by. As indicated, vehicles only occasionally pass on the road, serving our area.

After waiting over an hour, a vehicle finally arrived and transported her to the Nkawkaw hospital. Thankfully, she survived the near-death experience and returned home after about a week of hospitalization.

Then, my personal experience! When I reached Year 5 in primary school, I was struck by a mysterious ailment in my left ankle, which forced me to stay away from school for nearly two years. During this time, I underwent various treatments, some of which were quite horrendous.

**

The cumulative effects of my early experiences shaped my perspective and fueled my desire to contribute to improving the situation of my community.

As a child, I had pure and ambitious dreams. I wanted to help the less fortunate, enhance healthcare in my community, and combat poverty. I even imagined creating a mobile hospital to serve our little village and the surrounding settlements.

My desire to improve the healthcare situation in my community, along with my wish to understand the underlying causes of the illness that threatened my education, motivated me to pursue a degree in medicine.

Despite the challenges posed by my left ankle condition, I persevered and continued my education, eventually gaining admission to secondary school and later to sixth form.

I completed my sixth-form education in June 1978, anticipating admission to the University of Ghana Medical School in Accra that October. Unfortunately, due to unforeseen circumstances, I was not admitted as I had hoped. Although this was a setback, it did not deter me from pursuing my goal.

After a six-year struggle that involved traveling to Nigeria to work as a construction assistant and later as a teacher to save for my plane ticket to Germany, I finally enrolled at Hannover Medical School in the northern city of Hannover in October 1984.

With my admission to medical school, , I felt I was getting closer to realizing the childhood dreams and goals I had just referred to. However, it quickly became clear that significant funds would be required to achieve this aspiration. I began to ponder how I could raise the necessary money. I decided to turn to one of my passions: writing.

At this point, I want to take a moment to provide the reader with more details on the matter.

**

I discovered my passion for writing at an early age. In fact, I attempted to write my first novel when I was just 12 years old. Unfortunately, I wasn't able to complete it due to a lack of resources.

My first novel may not have been completed, but it didn't signal the end of my writing journey. Even during my secondary school days, I persisted in writing and contributed articles to our school magazine.

After secondary school, I continued to explore different forms of writing and submitted articles to the People's Evening News, a publication based in Accra.

My passion for writing was reignited when I moved to Germany. The change in environment sparked a new wave of creativity within me.

Indeed, the move from my impoverished African village to the affluent West ignited my passion for writing.

Imagine someone, perhaps much like yourself, with an insatiable passion for writing. Picture this individual growing up in a very poor and humble environment, only to later experience firsthand the thriving living conditions of affluent Western society.

Wow! I uncovered an endless array of themes to explore—such as the stark contrast between shops overflowing with goods here and the scarcity of items in my small village; the isolation experienced by individuals in the West compared to the open community of my village; and the weather—where some people are freezing in the cold while, back in my village, others are sweating under the heat.

Yes, indeed, I decided to highlight the wild world of extremely contradictory conditions, as exemplified by my little village, Mpintimpi, on the one side and Hannover, where I was cracking my brains to study medicine on the other.

I began to document the whirlwind of thoughts that raced through my mind as I observed my new surroundings. Whenever my busy schedule as a medical student allowed, I took the time to sit down and write my reflections.

As already indicated, my desire to write about my new environment from the point of view of a "little African village boy" was not only driven by my love for the craft but also by my determination to fulfil the long-held childhood dream: to improve the lives of the residents in my native village and its surroundings. I envisioned one of my books becoming a best-seller and imagined using part of the millions of dollars in income to help make that dream a reality.

Several months after I started writing about the starkly contrasting lifestyles of the small African village I had left behind and the affluent, sophisticated world I encountered in the West, I finished the manuscript for my first book, *The Call That Changed My Life*. In it, I shared my challenging journey from my hometown of Mpintimpi to my enrollment at Hanover Medical School.

While searching online for a publisher for my work, I came across a publishing service that assisted authors in self-publishing their books on a print-on-demand basis. I reached out to the owner, Charles who helped me edit my manuscript and prepare it for publication. Once the project was completed, I gave Charles, a complimentary copy of the book as a thank-you.

One day, he sent me a message saying, "Hi, Robert, I gave the book to one of my sons. He is excited and thinks it would make a good film!" While I appreciated the compliment, I didn't seriously consider pursuing the idea. I thought, "How could I come by the substantial amount of money it would take to produce a film?"

That was not the end of the matter. A year after the English edition was published, I released the German version. I rented a hall in Düsseldorf for the launch and gifted a copy of the book to the hall's owner. Not long after, I received a call from him.

"Hello, Robert. Let's meet to discuss the possibility of turning this book into a film. It is an exciting story that would make a great movie," he said. I agreed to the meeting.

Once I took my seat in his office, he began, "With your permission, I will present this book to a film company I know and discuss the prospect of adapting it into a film." Naturally, I did not object to the idea.

Shortly after our meeting, he sent a message to his associate recommending the book for adaptation into a film. I have yet to hear back from that individual.

**

As a passionate writer, I refused to put my pen down despite the setback and continued writing. I titled my second book A Letter to My Dying Mother. In this letter, sent to my gravely ill mother by a fictitious courier, I painted a vivid picture of the experiences she might have had if she had ever made it to the West during her lifetime.

**

Contrary to the popular belief that writing books can be a profitable venture, my experience in self-publishing has been a stark contrast. Unexpected financial losses have been a reality I've had to face.

As my accountant bluntly pointed out to me, "Your self-publishing activities have been hemorrhaging your earnings from your doctor's work."

Despite these financial setbacks, my passion for writing remains unwavering. It's this love for the craft that compels me to keep creating more titles, regardless of the challenges.

Over the years, I have written more than forty books, pouring my heart and soul into each one. Similar to my experience with *The Call that Changed My Life*, several readers of my other titles reached out, encouraging me to adapt them into films. However, like with *The Call that Changed My Life*, I consistently set aside these ideas due to financial constraints.

**

To mark the 40th anniversary of my arrival in Europe on May 12, 1982, in the middle of 2022, I published what I dubbed my African Duology—*Radical Therapy for Africa's Lookalike* and *Legacy Africa—Two Generations of Africans Confront The Problems of Continent Sunshine.*

The two novels encapsulated my thoughts on the challenges facing Africa and shared my vision for advancing Africa.

In *Radical Therapy for Africa's Lookalike*, I am called to heal a severely ailing patient who bears a striking resemblance to Africa. Drawing on my medical expertise, I take the patient's history and ultimately prescribe a cure.

Legacy Africa—Two Generations of Africans Confront The Problems of Continent Sunshine., which also stems from a dream experience, introduces Kwasi, a teenage boy of African descent whom I encounter on the streets of London. He appears troubled and shares that he has been feeling downhearted due to bullying from his classmates by virtue of his African heritage. As I try to uplift him, he is soon joined by his classmate Bola, a young girl also of African ancestry. I invite both of them to join me at a cafeteria in London, where we engage in a discussion about the challenges facing the continent and explore potential solutions.

**

In September 2023, I traveled to Ghana to launch both of my titles. I had invested countless hours and energy into pre-launch publicity, so I was deeply disappointed by the unexpectedly low turnout. I had dedicated significant time and effort to sharing my ideas with my fellow Africans, especially the youth, only to encounter a lack of interest.

Reflecting on the underwhelming launch of my two titles and the generally lackluster readership of my other books, I empathized with the shared struggle of many self-published and lesser-known authors. In a world inundated with an ever-growing number of books, gaining the desired readership is a formidable challenge.

The pervasive influence of social media significantly impacts this issue. While I don't have specific data to back this up, it's evident that many people today are more inclined to listen and watch rather than read.

Confronted with this reality, it dawned on me that adapting to current trends is not merely an option but a pressing necessity. Why should I spend thousands of hours writing only to see my message lost and forgotten in dusty books? To address this question, I decided that if no one was willing to read my books and understand the messages they contain, I would present the stories as films instead.

Thus, the idea of adapting my books into films surfaced once again. Readers may recall that I had previously dismissed this option due to financial concerns. However, this time, the desire to pursue filmmaking was too strong to ignore.

**

In my search for potential sources of funding for my plan, I turned to the Internet. One option that emerged from my research was crowdfunding. However, after careful consideration, I ultimately decided against pursuing this approach. Although I could potentially raise a few thousand pounds through crowdfunding, this amount would be insufficient to bring my project to fruition. This led me to question what I should do with the donations I received. Should I return the money to the donors? If I chose to do so, would it be feasible? With such thoughts in mind, I decided against pursuing crowdfunding for my filmmaking dreams. Instead, I chose to reach out to film producers who had previously worked on similar storylines, hoping they could connect me with potential investors.

Below is a reproduction of the letter I sent to about a dozen filmmakers I came across online.

Dear Sir/Madam

Allow me please to introduce myself. I am a medical doctor, a native of Ghana, currently residing in the UK. Growing up in a little village in Ghana, in one of the most impoverished settings on earth, I managed, by the hands of Providence, to make it to medical school in Germany.

I am a part-time doctor and also an author, evangelist, and human rights activist. Many of my books reflect the experiences of my formative years in my deprived village. In them, I address some of the challenges faced by people living in such impoverished communities.

I am eager to convert some of my books into movies. Through my online research, I understand the significant challenges of securing the necessary resources for a film project. Nevertheless, I have decided to pursue this goal. To this end, I am bringing two of my works to your attention and seeking your assistance in helping me realize my dream.

The titles involved are:

1. **WORLD WAR II REVISITED**—Memoirs of a Forced African Conscript ISBN:9780995552425 (2018)
2. **POVERTY CRUSADE**—A Little African Village's Campaign against world poverty ISBN: 9781913285005 (2019)

I have included brief summaries of both titles in this letter. I would greatly appreciate any assistance you can provide to help me achieve my goal. I look forward to hearing from you at your earliest convenience.

Yours sincerely
R.P.-G.

I sent the letter to several prominent film producers, but I did not receive any responses.

**

Even though my efforts did not yield the desired results, my strong wish to adapt some of my books into films persisted.

One of my personal philosophies is that if you venture into the unknown, you may succeed or fail. On the other hand, if you decide not to venture, failure is already assured.

Without trying to overstate matters, I must say I have, on several occasions in my life, not shunned venturing into the unknown—yes, engaging in audacious ventures into the unknown.

I will cite only three instances:

In December 1980, I left Ghana and headed for Nigeria, not knowing where I would stay on my arrival. I aimed to work there to earn the money needed to pay for my journey to Germany to fulfil my goal of studying medicine.

In May 1982, after spending around 16 months in Nigeria, I left Lagos and headed for the then West Berlin. As I left, I was unsure where I would spend the first night on my arrival in Europe—for I had neither a visa for Germany nor did I know anyone to lodge with.

In 2006, when my solo medical practice in Germany was nearing bankruptcy, I relocated to the UK to work in a new environment and practice medicine within an unfamiliar system.

As I pursued my desire to adapt some of my books into films, with limited financial resources and minimal knowledge of film production, I was driven by the same bold spirit that had fueled my determination in the past.

Once again, I was stepping into an uncertain future. Without funding from external sources, I would have to rely on my own means. I couldn't help but wonder what would happen if things didn't go as planned and I faced personal bankruptcy. Despite those concerns lingering in my mind, I chose to set them aside and pursue my goal, no matter the obstacles that might arise.

**

As previously stated, I have written over 40 books. Many of them could be adapted into films, so I asked myself which book I should start my filmmaking journey with.

After careful consideration, I decided to begin with LEGACY AFRICA. Readers might wonder why I made this choice, so here are my reasons:

First and foremost, I considered the economics. As already mentioned, in the book, I had the opportunity to meet two African teenagers. I invited them to a café to discuss some of Africa's challenges and brainstorm potential strategies for overcoming them.

I concluded that the simplicity of the storyline would allow for a low-cost film adaptation. Furthermore, I expected that it would require only a few cast members, which would further reduce the cost of hiring actors. To keep expenses even further down, I decided to portray myself in the film—essentially; I would take on my own role!

**

How did you feel you were suited to play your role? Readers might wonder. Before answering the question, I want to take the reader to my secondary school days.

From 1971 to 1976, I was a boarder at the Oda Secondary School in Akim Oda, a town about 120 kilometres northwest of Accra, Ghana's capital.

During my time at Odasco, as we referred to our school for short, I became a member of the Dramatic Society.

I no longer recall the circumstances that led me to join the society.

Was it a choice I made, or was I assigned a role by our English teacher who was also a patron of the society? The answer remains a mystery, lost in the annals of time.

I was not just a passive member of the performing club; I also participated in a handful of plays that we enacted to entertain the entire school.

While not trying to sing my praises, I was not considered a lousy actor based on the remarks I received from some of my peers after watching our performances.

Was my involvement with the Dramatic Society at my alma mater a way Providence prepared me for the role I assumed in LEGACY AFRICA? Well, I can only speculate.

So, despite the odds, I was determined to venture into film production. I was, as it were, ready to cross the Rubicon.

Chapter 2

The ABCs of Film Production

After deciding to turn Legacy Africa into a film, I started outlining the steps necessary to achieve this goal. My first action was to research film production online. Below is a brief overview of what I learned. This overview is not meant to be a comprehensive guide to filmmaking; rather, it serves as a starting point for further research and learning. Those interested in gaining a more detailed understanding should refer to relevant resources.

Most importantly, I learned that the key players in a film production project are not just job titles, but essential contributors to the creative process. They are listed below:

PRODUCER
DIRECTOR
CAST
CREW

The crew on its part consists of the following:

Camera Department.
Lighting and Grip Department.
Sound Department.
Art Department
Wardrobe, Hair, and Makeup.

I will briefly outline the roles of the individuals and departments mentioned above.

PRODUCER: A film producer bears the responsibility of the entire production, overseeing every stage from concept to final cut. This role involves organizing script readings, meticulously scheduling shooting days, carefully budgeting for all aspects of production, selecting and hiring the cast and crew, strategically marketing to potential distributors, and overseeing the distribution process. The producer is the driving force that brings the project to life, transforming it from a mere idea into a tangible reality.

DIRECTOR: In summary, a film director is responsible for overseeing the artistic and dramatic elements of a movie. They interpret the screenplay and guide both the film crew and the actors to bring that vision to life. In other words, the director serves as the creative eye for the entire film production team.

CAST: The cast is a group of actors who bring a film's storyline to life on stage. They are, as it were, the heart and soul of a film or stage play.

Acting roles come in various forms, including lead actors, supporting actors, and extras. The complexities of these roles are intriguing and deserve exploration, but they are beyond the scope of this book.

CREW: I just highlighted the role of the cast in a film. The cast performs to bring the film to life. The crew on their part, are the professionals who work behind the scenes to create a movie. These include the following:

CINEMATOGRAPHER: The cinematographer, also known as the director of photography (DP), plays a crucial role on a film set. In a small production like Legacy Africa, the cinematographer's responsibilities are extensive. They are in charge of the photography aspect, ensuring the camera is set up to capture the perfect shot.

In larger film productions with multiple cameras, the cinematographer's role expands beyond just capturing individual shots; they also oversee the work of various camera operators. Depending on the size of the set, the cinematographer may have one or a few assistants to help with these tasks.

SOUND: As I researched online for a crew for Legacy Africa, two terms that fascinated me the most were Boom Operator and Gaffer.

Boom Operator—what type of role does he fulfil? I wondered.

The term, which initially sounded like a foreign language, turned out to be a fascinating discovery—it referred to the audio engineer, a specialist in live recording. The boom operator assists in the production by operating boom microphones, selecting and placing radio microphones, and maintaining the audio equipment.

GAFFER: I just made mention of my fascination for the terminology Gaffer

The Gaffer, as I learned, is briefly put, **the** chief lighting technician or the head electrician responsible for executing the lighting plan for a production

MAKE-UP ARTIST: The makeup artist on a film set is responsible for creating and applying makeup to actors, enhancing their appearance to match the character's personality and the overall visual style of the film. This role includes designing character looks, ensuring makeup continuity throughout filming, and sometimes applying special effects makeup

**

STAGES IN FILM PRODUCTION: After highlighting the film production team and their various roles, I would now consider the different stages in film production. These are as follows:

1. Development
2. Pre-Production
3. Production
4. Post-Production
5. Distribution/Marketing

I want to briefly shed light on each of these stages.

Development: This stage includes generating, writing, and organizing ideas for the project.

Pre-production: This stage focuses on planning and executing all tasks before filming.

Production: This is the stage where the actual filming of the movie occurs.

Post-production: This stage of the filmmaking process involves editing footage, adding music and sound effects, and enhancing visuals to improve the film.

Distribution: This is the final stage of film production, where the finished film is promoted and released to audiences.

Chapter 3A

The making of Legacy Africa: European Segment

After providing a broad overview of the basics of film production, I will now discuss how I applied the insights gained to facilitate the production of Legacy Africa.

DEVELOPMENT: As stated above, the developmental stage of a film involves generating, writing, and organizing ideas for the project. The financial aspect is also considered at this stage.

From my research on the topic, I discovered that established film production companies invest significant time at the beginning of a project to develop a thorough filming budget, carefully accounting for every aspect before moving forward.

As I mentioned at the onset, I did not write "Legacy Africa" with the intention of adapting it into a film.

However, when the compelling idea to adapt it into a film came to me, I faced a significant challenge: I didn't have substantial funds available.

"How are you able to come by the necessary funds for the project?" I kept asking myself.

Unable to keep my thoughts to myself, I decided to share my ideas with the rest of the family towards the end of December 2023.

"I am seriously considering adapting my book *Legacy Africa* into a film," I announced, filled with determination.

"Say that again," one of them responded, clearly astonished.

"Yes, you heard me right!" I stated.

"How do you finance it? How do you market it? Be aware that countless films are out there competing for viewers!" one of them remarked.

The meeting revealed that the rest of my family had serious doubts about the feasibility of the proposal. On the surface, their concerns were valid. I didn't have even a fraction of the required funds in my bank account. But as a born optimist—or perhaps a crazy dreamer?—I was resolute in pursuing the venture despite the financial challenge.

**

After deciding to produce Legacy Africa, my first priority was to adapt the book into a screenplay. I considered enrolling in a screenplay course to learn the necessary skills to write the script myself. However, a voice within me warned, "Don't try to be a jack of all trades and a master of none!"

Given my busy schedule as a general practitioner and an author (I was working on a manuscript at the time), I realized that the quickest way to convert the book into a screenplay would be to entrust the task to someone else—someone with the expertise I lacked.

To find a ghostwriter, I began researching online. Eventually, I discovered a service provider based in Nigeria, and I felt she was the right person for the job. Not only did she have excellent reviews, but her African background, cultural insights, and personal experiences would add authenticity to the screenplay I envisioned.

About two months after I submitted the manuscript, Diana—her first name—delivered the script. She did an outstanding job transforming the book into a vibrant screenplay—a true masterpiece!

PRE-PRODUCTION: With the screenplay complete, I started to assemble the production team. At this point, I encountered an important issue that I had not previously considered: the challenge of producing a film across two continents, Europe and Africa.

While a well-established producer with a large budget could cover the costs of relocating the entire team between continents, I realized that this was not feasible for an amateur producer like myself, who had limited funds.

In the end I opted to work with separate crews for each continent.

**

At this juncture, I would like to introduce a section of the London production team.

Producer: Though I did not wish it for myself, by virtue of my role as the initiator and also the main source of financing, I earned the title of producer of the project.

When I travelled to Ghana to join the filming team, everyone referred to me as the Executive Producer. Thus the Ghana team elevated me from a ***mere*** Producer to an Executive Producer.

Director: My role had been established; the next crucial position that needed filling was that of the director. Yes, indeed, I needed to find a director for the film.

Even before I began my research into film-making, I knew that the director plays a key role in a film. How often have I watched the TV news reporting about Hollywood Oscars going to directors of this and that film? So, with a sense of anticipation, I began to look for a director.

Who would assume that key role? I began to wonder.

As I contemplated the matter, I went to work at an outpatient facility in a hospital in a city not far from my residence to meet a patient by the first name of Eric who had moved from Ghana to the UK not long before our meeting. As I engaged him in a conversation, he revealed that he had directed a couple of short and feature films in Ghana.

"That is exactly the kind of person I am looking for," I said, giving him a broad outline of the film project I was planning.

Initially, I assigned Eric the role of Director.

However, the arrangement was short-lived. As I noted earlier, he had just settled in the UK and faced personal challenges in adapting to his new environment. These challenges affected his ability to provide the focus and dedication needed for such an undertaking.

As a first step towards finding a replacement for Eric, I posted a notice on Backstage. Eventually, I found someone who had the qualifications and skills for the job.

Just as I was celebrating my new director, he sent me a message , just a week prior to the filming , to cancel our engagement due to a family emergency.

The cancellation of the newly-found director, which as just indicated happened just a few days before the filming date, threatened to derail everything.

With the filming arrangements already in place—the location secured, and the crew and equipment hired—any rescheduling would not only create a logistical nightmare but also incur a hefty price tag, potentially jeopardizing the project's budget.

As I faced the looming crisis, Richard, our resourceful production manager, came to the rescue.

"Wait a minute. I will call someone I know who can help. He directed a successful film, and I hope he is available," he began.

"Go ahead and call him, Richard; things are getting precarious," I responded.

Fortunately, Mania, the individual in question, a seasoned director experienced in navigating such challenges, was available and eager to step in.

Production Manager: Richard, who I just referred to, has been a dedicated force in the project. A native of Uganda, I first met him in London over a decade before my venture into filming. Over the last several years, he has served as my videographer, pouring his passion into producing a good number of short videos for my YouTube channel.

While he wasn't formally recruited to serve as the production manager, Richard's significant role in coordinating the London filming rightfully earned him that designation.

I would like to highlight some of the key roles he played in facilitating the filming in London.

Firstly, he leveraged his connections with a local church to secure a hall for our auditions, which we later used for rehearsals as well.

Additionally, he was crucial in recruiting staff to assist with logistics and security on the filming day. Richard also took the lead in organizing the meals and drinks for the filming team.

**

The script was complete, and despite my limited financial resources, I was determined to move forward. The next step was to recruit the cast.

As I stated above, I decided to play my role.

How, then, do I come across the remaining cast?

Once again, I went online to research the matter. In the process, I chanced upon Backstage, an online platform for recruiting cast members, crew, and performing artists.

After registering and paying a fee, I posted a notice to recruit the two key characters, Kwasi and Bola.

I was pleasantly surprised by the overwhelming response to the advertisement. Although the notice indicated that the event would take place in London, I received applications from candidates as far away as the US and Canada.

As I communicated with applicants outside the UK to inform them of their unsuccessful applications, I was reminded of a time in my own life when I experienced a series of rejection letters.

Fresh out of medical school, I was in desperate need of a placement for my post-graduate training. The job market in Germany was saturated with junior doctors, making it extremely difficult to secure a hospital placement for my specialization.

While the majority of applicants I turned down seemed to have accepted the situation, one applicant from New York appeared quite disappointed and frustrated. She made me believe that she was willing to fly to London for the audition!

After pre-selecting a group of candidates for the roles of Kwasi and Bola, I posted a few additional notices on Backstage to find actors for the remaining roles. These included Kwasi's classmates, who bullied him because of his African background, and my German anatomy professor.

**

AUDITION ISSUES: As I was putting up notices to find my actors, someone mentioned that I needed to hold auditions to select suitable candidates.

"Audition? What is that?" I asked.

I was informed that an audition involves setting a date, preparing a script for the actors to perform, and arranging a panel to judge their performances.

For those familiar with the world of theatre, my lack of knowledge about the term may come as a surprise. However, for me, it was a new concept—a part of the learning process I was about to begin.

With the help of Richard, I booked a hall in London for the audition. Once the venue was secured, I promptly sent out invitations to the first group of actors auditioning for the roles of Bola and Kwasi. The event took place on Saturday, January 27, 2024.

All the attendees, mainly in their late teens and early twenties, demonstrated remarkable enthusiasm, making it challenging to choose among them.

Regrettably, we had to make some difficult decisions and turn down a few attendees. I encouraged those who were not selected to stay hopeful, assuring them that they would be considered for other roles

The selection process not only fulfilled its main goal of identifying the right individuals for the team but also provided me with valuable insights into human behavior.

Some individuals who attended the selection were flexible in their approach. Even though they did not secure the roles they applied for, they were still pleased to accept my offer to join the team in other capacities, such as supporting actors. In contrast, others adopted a take-it-or-leave-it attitude. They either insisted on being assigned the lead role or chose not to participate.

**

I do not need to give a lecture here. When watching a war film, for example, one can see numerous soldiers on screen. Though they are not strictly part of the main cast, their contributions are invaluable.

The film features a scene where I am depicted as a solitary African student sitting in a lecture hall with my year group, which consists of around three hundred students, predominantly German nationals. To accurately represent this scene, I needed to hire several actors of European descent to fill the lecture hall.

In another scene, I was seated with Kwasi and Bola, sharing a meal in a cafeteria. It goes without saying that we weren't alone in the restaurant; we needed a lively atmosphere to make the scene come to life.

Similar to my search for actors with specific roles, I recruited Extras through Backstage. Unlike the main actors, I didn't need to hold auditions. I simply invited anyone interested to join us on the filming day.

While the participation of the Extras was crucial for the scenes, it created a significant logistical challenge. The expenses for transportation, meals, and daily fees for the sizeable number of Extras had a considerable impact on the production budget.

**

THE LONDON CREW: It is superfluous to mention that I recruited all the crew needed for the London filming with the help of Backstage,

**

The cinematographer. After reading his profile, I initially settled on Angus. He had moved from Hong Kong to the UK and made an excellent impression on me.

Just a few days before the filming, however, he messaged me with shocking news-he had to rush back to Hong Kong due to a family emergency, throwing an unexpected challenge our way.

Happily, Angus did not leave us in limbo. Instead, he introduced us to Molin, who happily had an availability for us.

Molin turned out to be not just highly experienced, but also incredibly dedicated. His commitment to the project reassured us and instilled confidence in our team's ability to handle unexpected situations.

Sound Engineer: We organized two separate filming sessions in London, and on each occasion, I had to hire a different sound engineer. George, with his unique perspective and passion for sound engineering, was a perfect fit for our team. His experience was evident, and his dedication significantly elevated the overall quality of our film, making the first session a memorable experience.

George was unavailable for the second session. Joan stepped into George's role and delivered an equally outstanding performance, showcasing the team's adaptability and professionalism.

Lightning: Nikitas, was responsible for the Lightning Department and was available for both sessions in London. He demonstrated a strong sense of dedication and duty towards his role.

Make-Up Artist: I hired a talented makeup artist. She did an excellent job, transforming my appearance and making me look several years younger.

**

I had already assembled the cast and crew for the project, I needed to secure equipment .

I aimed high. Even though finances were tight, I was determined to create a film that could meet the standards of top streaming platforms.

With limited experience, I initially considered purchasing a camera, its accessories, and other gadgets necessary for filmmaking.

However, I quickly realized that the prices for cameras and lenses that would meet the requirements of streaming platforms were far beyond my budget.

Eventually, I decided to follow the advice of Paul, a videographer who had previously given me some basic training in film production. He suggested that I rent the set of equipment instead of purchasing them.

While the cost of renting did impact our budget, it was a significant relief to find a solution that was much more affordable than buying outright.

**

While I was recruiting the cast and crew and making inquiries about the equipment, I also considered the filming locations.

As mentioned earlier, the film has two geographical settings: Africa and Europe.

The European locations consist of two distinct segments: the vibrant city of London (UK) and the charming city of Hannover (Germany).

I will return to the African location later in the narrative; for now, I will focus on the European segment.

The London segment includes the following scenes:

- The Garden scene, where I meet Kwasi and Bola.
- The cafeteria scene, where I invite them to lunch.
- A hall where I address a meeting of the African Youth Alliance.

The Hannover segment includes:

- My arrival at Hannover airport to begin my medical studies.
- I, a lone student of African descent, seated in a lecture hall with around 300 students, mainly German nationals.
- I, strolling around the city center of Hannover.

My initial approach to searching for locations revealed my complete inexperience in this area.

As a novice in the intricate world of filming, I initially thought that scenes should be shot in the exact locations described in the script. For example, I thought the lecture hall scene should take place at my alma mater, while the domino restaurant scene should be filmed in a typical domino outlet.

With this in mind, I began calling various Domino restaurants in and around London to seek their permission to film in one of their outlets. Eventually, someone advised me to contact their headquarters directly. I followed their suggestion and sent a letter to the London HQ.

For a while, I didn't receive any response, and I can't blame them—the letter was returned by Royal Mail because the stamp I had used was no longer valid. They even considered charging me a surcharge for the return, but ultimately, they dropped the letter in my mailbox without insisting on the surcharge.

I didn't attempt to resend the letter, and the reason for that will soon become clear.

Around the time I sent letters to the Domino office in the UK, I also emailed the relevant authorities at my alma mater to explain my situation and request permission to film a scene in the lecture hall at the medical school. The university kindly declined my request, stating that it no longer allowed commercial filming within its halls. However, they offered a compromise: I could film at the entrance and the adjacent area.

How can I find a suitable lecture hall to film my scene? I wondered. As I had done on previous occasions, I went online to research the options. I was pleasantly surprised to discover that many agencies specialize in securing filming locations for filmmakers. The possibilities are endless, making it incredibly easy to hire spaces for virtually any type of scene—cafeterias, restaurants, hospitals, churches, and more. I was particularly intrigued to learn that it's even possible to rent an entire school or college campus for filming. With this new insight, I decided not to send a second letter to Domino's and instead explore potential options through these agencies.

I decided to prioritize a college location to film the London scene. My preference was based on the following considerations: A college campus offered us the unique opportunity to capture almost all the London components of the filming—park, classroom, cafeteria, etc.—in one place.

After exploring a couple of options available online, we were thrilled to settle on a college in South East London, a location that promised to bring our vision to life.

The fee charged was far beyond what I had budgeted, forcing me to book it for only one day. In hindsight, we had better reserve it for two consecutive days—more later.

Another expense I had not initially envisaged was the need to purchase Public Liability Insurance, which exerted further pressure on already strained resources.

**

Before I move on to the production stage, I would like to briefly report on the rehearsals. I'm not sure how many rehearsal sessions established production companies typically conduct before filming, but we decided to hold two sessions.

While some actors requested payment for participating in the rehearsals, the majority were satisfied with reimbursement for their transportation costs and the complimentary meals provided.

I previously mentioned my acting experience at Oda Secondary School, where I performed in various plays. The situation I found myself in as I returned to acting was quite different from my time in secondary school. Back then, I was in my adolescent years, full of energy and possessing a sharp mind that made it easy for me to learn and memorize lines.

Now, however, age has taken its toll on my cognitive abilities. As a busy general practitioner, author, and someone involved in various other activities, I struggled to find the time needed for memorization.

How did I address the challenge? I went online to search for devices and resources to help me overcome the challenge. One device I considered was an ear prompter. This two-way device consists of one part that is inserted into the inner ear, while the other connects to a recorder. The ear prompter is praised for its ability to allow individuals to deliver their lines word for word, eliminating the need for memorization or holding a script.

Although I found the concept appealing, I ultimately decided against it. My research indicated that these devices are not mass-produced; it seemed that one would need to assemble the components and find someone to install them. Additionally, I was uncertain about how to prevent the audience from noticing the device during my performance.

In the end, I resorted to the following method to help me master my lines:

I recorded the lines on my mobile phone and played them back whenever I was alone, in particular when I went alone on a walk. I lived close to a forest, and my custom was to go for regular walks there. On such occasions, I listened to the recordings—often without resorting to an earphone. Occasionally, the curious, wondering glances of passersby would be directed at me.

Unexpectedly, this method proved to be very effective. During rehearsals and filming, I recited my lines, even the longer ones, with relative ease, much to the astonishment of my director and younger acting colleagues.

**

LONDON FILMING DAY 1

Finally, the much-awaited filming day, May 31, 2024, arrived. As a first-timer in filming, I couldn't help but wonder—will everything unfold as planned?

No, they didn't. It all began with the filming of the first scene of the day. Having paid a considerable fee for the location, a college campus as already stated, I thought we had access to the entire premises. However, our access was actually limited to a specific section of the property, as stated in the contract.

Unfortunately, amid the hectic, I hadn't taken the time to read the fine print!

Molin, our diligent cinematographer conducted location scouting three days before filming and was drawn to two potential sites. He found it challenging to choose between them.

On the day of filming, he arrived before I did and ultimately decided on a classroom, which, as it turned out, was not specified in the contract.

Unaware of these contractual limitations, as he had not read the contract, he made his decision based on the aesthetics and practicality of the selected classroom. The school had assigned a chaperone to ensure that our filming proceeded smoothly. When the chaperone noticed our breach of contract, he promptly reported the situation to his superior, who rushed to the site to verify what was happening.

Realizing that filming was already in progress, the superior decided not to interrupt us. However, he delivered a stern warning: "You have not adhered to the terms of the contract. This will likely have significant financial repercussions." It indeed turned out to be a costly mistake on our part, and we would come to realize just how much later on.

However, the hoopla surrounding the mix-up did not rattle our diligent cinematographer, dutiful director, and the rest of the team. Instead, we remained composed and diligently executed the filming schedule for the day as planned.

**

The team decided to start the filming session with what we referred to as "the bullying scene," in which Kwasi's friends taunt him because of his African heritage.

As someone new to the world of filming, I assumed they would finish the scene in just a few minutes. However, I quickly learned that the complexity of the process was far greater than I anticipated.

Coming from a medical background, where surgeons aim to complete procedures swiftly to minimize a patient's exposure to anesthesia, I found the world of filming to be a stark contrast.

It was a swift realization that the 'one and done' principle, which I was accustomed to in other areas of life, was not applicable to the intricate process of filming a set.

**

"One, two, three, action!" the director would call out, only to shout moments later, "Cut! Quiet, please! Restart!"

This start-stop-restart cycle became a never-ending pattern, highlighting the slow pace of filming. As a result, what I thought should be a straightforward process dragged on at a snail's pace, leading to frustration and impatience on the part of the medical doctor turned film producer!

Ultimately, the first scene, which would only have a few minutes of screen time, took nearly two hours to complete. This might not bother professionals in the industry, but for a layperson like me, it was a learning experience.

Another cause of concern, as I witnessed the slow progress unfolding before me, was that since I was venturing into film production with limited resources, I was determined to avoid getting stuck in the middle of the project with exhausted resources.

**

Next, the crew set out to film a pivotal scene we referred to as 'the lecture hall scene.' This scene, which primarily focused on me, was a crucial part of the film's narrative.

We captured a compelling storyline in the film: "I was the only person of African descent among a year group of 300, mostly German students."

More than three decades have passed since the events we were reenacting. My once deep black hair has turned grey, and my smooth face has developed wrinkles. It was a moment of deep personal reflection, pondering over who could help me regain my youthful appearance.

The task was assigned to Alice, the makeup artist I mentioned earlier. After a session that lasted about half an hour, she used her professional skills to make me look several years younger. It was truly a remarkable transformation.

Filming the 'Lecture Hall' scene was a significant undertaking that felt like it stretched on endlessly, at least from my perspective. Brigitte's professionalism in portraying Professor Schmidt, my German anatomy professor, was commendable. Despite the need for multiple takes, she maintained her focus and delivered the 'lecture' with precision, which earned my admiration.

The dedication of the Extras who filled the lecture hall, stepping into the roles of my German classmates, was truly remarkable. Despite the language barrier, they remained attentive and engaged, bringing the scene to life.

After a dedicated effort of about two hours, we finally wrapped up the challenging lecture hall scene. I looked at my watch and realized it was a few minutes past one o'clock. The pressure of my ambitious schedule began to weigh heavily on me. I had planned to film all the London scenes in a single day, a task that felt increasingly daunting as I recognized that we had only managed to complete two out of the seven-plus scenes. The thought of extending my budget for another day of filming sent shivers down my spine.

Noticing my nervousness, my diligent director reassured me that he would do his best to stick to the day's schedule.

**

The director had planned to move on to the next scene immediately upon completion of the "Lecture Hall" scene. However, our hunger and the need for a break were undeniable. The entire team, including myself, was united in expressing a desire for a lunch break, a necessary pause in our intense filming schedule.

"Okay, everyone, please wait for me while I pick up the food I ordered from a nearby restaurant," said Richard, the production manager. His steadfast commitment to his responsibilities even when faced with unexpected delays, was truly commendable and demonstrated his dedication to his work.

**

After the lunch break, we carefully moved the gadgets and equipment from the lecture hall to the college cafeteria to prepare for "the cafeteria scene." By around 3 p.m., we were ready to start filming. In this scene, I shared a meal with Kwasi and Bola as we discussed Africa's challenges and explored potential solutions. It took us approximately 90 minutes to complete the scene.

After 5 p.m., the director instructed everyone to head to a hall where the next scene was scheduled to be filmed. This scene involved me addressing a meeting of the Africa Youth Alliance, a Pan-African youth organization.

We began filming the African Youth Association scene under significant time constraints. The terms of our location rental required us to vacate the premises by 7 p.m. at the latest.

Not only was our filming schedule tight in relation to this deadline, but the company from which we hired the filming equipment had originally promised to pick up the items by 6:30 p.m. However, they called us an hour before their scheduled arrival to inform us that, due to unforeseen circumstances, they would be an hour late.

As the filming of the Africa Youth Alliance meeting ended just minutes before our 7 p.m. deadline, we found ourselves in a high-stakes race against time. Desperate to beat the deadline, we hurriedly dismantled our equipment in the main building and transported it to the parking lot, believing we would fulfil our contractual obligations once we left the main school compound and congregated there.

We miscalculated, as it turned out, because they quickly pointed out that waiting in the parking lot counted as over-staying our allocated time. Ultimately, they charged us an extra fee for this overstay and for using a part of the prem-ises that was not specified in the original contract to film the "bullying scene."

These unexpected expenses, which were not accounted for in my already tight budget, put a significant strain on my financial resources.

Despite the misfortune, I found solace in the realization that the first filming day had gone well. Mistakes had been made, but they were part of the learning process in my new role as a film producer, and they would only make me bet-ter in the future.

**

When I was arranging the London filming, a thought crossed my mind: It would be wise to consider two filming days and hire the location and the production team for two consecutive days instead of one.

Due to my lack of experience in the industry, I made the overly optimistic assumption that we could complete filming in a single day.

As I headed home from the first filming day, having accomplished just about half of the schedule, I was filled with regret. My over-optimism had cost me more than just time. It would also cost me money—money that would have been saved if I had planned for two consecutive days of filming from the beginning.

**

Organizing a second day of filming from scratch was a significant challenge. It involved a thorough search for a new outdoor location that met the specific requirements for the remaining scenes. I decided not to rehire the location used for Day 1 filming due to the nature of these scenes.

Additionally, I had to rehire the production crew and equipment, cover extra fees for the cast, pay for transportation costs, and provide meals and drinks for everyone during the shoot.

**

R. Peprah-Gyamfi

LONDON FILMING DAY 2

Saturday, June 29, 2024, the day for filming the remaining London scenes, finally arrived.

Aside from the sound engineer who could not attend due to his commitment at Glastonbury, a major summer music festival in the UK, the crew for Day 2 of filming was the same as Day 1. We brought in Joan, another sound engineer, whose expertise greatly benefited our team.

The cast for Day 2 was considerably smaller than on Day 1. It consisted of myself, Bola, Kwasi, and two young women who portrayed Bola's classmates. Unlike the first day of filming, which was held indoors, the scenes on Day 2 took place entirely outdoors, primarily in a public park.

I had initially thought that filming outside in a public park would not incur a fee. To be cautious, I contacted the relevant authorities. However, they informed me that this was not the case. We were required not only to apply for permission but also to present a public liability insurance policy before our application could be considered.

After fulfilling all the necessary requirements and paying for four hours of filming time, we were excited to start our project in the public park from 10 a.m. to 2 p.m.

Since we had paid to film in the park, I assumed the authorities would post a notice to inform the public and request that they stay away from the area during our reserved time. To our surprise, no such notice was posted.

In fact, we had barely arrived and begun to set up when several individuals started to flood into the area. And it wasn't just people; many of the newcomers brought their four-legged companions—dogs—which added an unexpected challenge to our filming!

When we moved from Germany to the UK in 2006, my first impression was that the residents of our new home preferred cats over dogs. I reached this conclusion because I encountered more people with cats than with dogs.

It's interesting to note the shift in pet preferences in the UK over the years. I have observed a growing fondness for dogs among the population. Nowadays, I meet many more individuals accompanied by dogs, which starkly contrasts with my initial impression of a cat-loving nation.

My observations on the second filming day further confirmed my suspicion. Almost every individual or family that arrived at the location was accompanied by a dog. It was a remarkable sight, with more than half a dozen dogs of various sizes and breeds, reinforcing the change in pet preferences I had noticed.

The presence of many dogs reminded me of an unpleasant experience I had not long before that day. I had the routine of going for walks in a park not far from our residence. On one occasion, as I stopped at the edge of the forest and contemplated the clouds in the skies, I turned to look around only to realize two dangerous dogs had taken their positions near me. As my eyes made contact with one of them, it began barking aggressively. The second dog soon joined in! I stood still, feeling the tension rise. Moments later, the owner arrived, bringing a wave of relief to me. " You did the right thing by staying calm, Mate," The owner reassured me and tried to silence the barking dogs, but the canines continued their vocal protest for a while longer.

What was to be done? We could not film in peace without being distracted by the newcomers, so at the suggestion of one team member, we approached the newcomers to explain our situation.

Upon hearing our explanation, the park visitors demonstrated their understanding and quickly relocated to the far end of the park. Their cooperation was instrumental in allowing us to proceed with our work without further disruption.

Since we were filming outdoors, we were mainly at the mercy of the weather. Those familiar with UK weather know it can be pretty unpredictable, even in the middle of summer. This unpredictability added an extra layer of uncertainty to our filming.

Contrary to our concerns, we were fortunate to have a beautiful summer day, which allowed us to accomplish our filming schedule without any weather-related interruptions.

Thus, aside from the minor issue with park visitors and their dogs, the filming session went smoothly, enabling us to wrap up reasonably well ahead of our 2 PM deadline.

**

FILMING IN HANNOVER, GERMANY

The northern German city of Hannover, the capital of the German Federal State of Lower Saxony, holds a special place in my heart. It was at the prestigious Hannover Medical School where I realized my dream of studying to become a doctor.

But Hannover's influence in my life doesn't stop there. It was in the bustling heart of Hannover, at the central train station, that I met Rita, who would eventually become my wife. And it was in the same city that all three of our children began their earthly journey, surrounded by the warmth and family values that Hannover embodies.

How can I film "Legacy Africa," a project that addresses the challenges facing Africa while also reflecting my personal journey, without including elements from Hannover?

After completing the filming in London, I made plans to travel to the northern German city to capture aspects of my time there.

Where would be the best spot to capture my arrival in the city to begin my studies, aside from the airport? I sent an email to the airport authorities requesting permission to film there. Initially, I anticipated encountering bureaucratic hurdles, such as being asked for evidence of public liability insurance coverage. However, I was pleasantly surprised by their response. Unlike in London, where I had to provide public liability insurance and pay to use various locations, they allowed me to film without such requirements. Their only condition was that I film in public areas while avoiding security zones.

Next, I needed to find a cinematographer who could use a camera that produced results similar to those we had used in London. I once again turned to the Internet and posted my requirements on several platforms. In response, I received around half a dozen replies. After carefully evaluating factors such as availability, cost, and the quality of their previous work, I decided to go with Mathias.

We began our filming journey at the airport, then moved to the tranquil environment of the medical school, and finally arrived at the busy city center. Each location provided a unique backdrop for our silent scenes, contributing a variety of visuals to our project.

How could I film my time in Hannover without including the Kropke Uhr (Kropke Clock)? This iconic landmark, a large clock encased in a green metal box just a few hundred metres from the central railway station, has woven itself into the fabric of Hannover's culture and history. It's a popular meeting point for various occasions—lovers rendezvousing for a date, business associates arranging a meeting, strangers meeting for the first time, and more.

After approximately five hours of careful planning and execution, we captured the highlights of my time in the city at three key locations: the airport, the medical school, and the city center.

Chapter 3B

The making of Legacy Africa: African Segment

Having successfully captured the European filming scenes, we turned our attention to the equally exciting Ghana segment.

I had hoped to use the same crew for the filming in Ghana; however, this was not possible due to previously discussed reasons. As a result, we needed to assemble an entirely new team for the production in Ghana.

**

Before I delve deeper into the narration of the filming experience in Ghana, I will briefly introduce some key members of the Ghana team.

Joseph

I chose Joseph, the son of my brother Thomas, to assume the role of my special assistant. One might find it intriguing that I speak of Joseph as my son rather than my nephew. To shed light on this unique aspect, I briefly explain a fascinating facet of our Akan tradition relating to familial relationships.

In our culture, I regard my brothers' children as my own children and not my nephews or nieces. Following the dictates of this tradition, the children of my brothers refer to me as their Dad or Papa.

However, the situation is different when it comes to the children of my sisters. According to our tradition, they are indeed my nieces and nephews and refer to me as their uncle. I don't want to delve any deeper into the nuances of the tradition so as not to digress entirely from the theme of this book.

Joseph was assigned diverse responsibilities related to the project. His role was truly multifaceted.

Among other things, he organized the Ghana audition, led the team to scout the production site, planned the production team's boarding and lodging at the various filming locations, and served as the financial secretary.

I strategically decided to entrust him with negotiating the fees of the various crew members and ancillary staff required for the filming, keeping the following considerations in mind. Among the Ghanaian populace (this may be true of nationals of other African countries), it is generally held that those who have left our shores to seek greener pastures in the West are generally wealthy. The fact that I was not only returning from the West but was also a medical doctor raised expectations even higher.

Aware of my background, I could imagine those I approached directly to hire, calling exaggerated and exorbitant fees.

The strategy worked, for he managed to bargain down the initial sums various parties demanded to about eighty per cent of the original quotes in many instances.

Director "Godfidence"

The screenplay involved filming approximately 80% of the scenes in Ghana, with the remainder shot in London and Hannover.

For reasons that the reader is already familiar with, I chose to use two completely different teams for filming the European and African segments of the production.

How do I find a competent person to direct the Ghana production?

Readers will remember Eric, an early candidate for the position of director of London production. He recommended one of his associates in Ghana. Joseph established initial contact with him. Even before we could discuss his application, Joseph called me one day and recommended Confidence.

"How did you get to know him?" I queried.

"I first met him during my teenage years while living in Tema. He was creating what I would describe as amateur films. Although I don't recall the exact circumstances of our initial meeting, he ended up offering me roles in several of his movies!"

"Really?"

"Yes indeed!"

"Do you have any clips to share?"

"Oh, that was very long ago. It was in the era of the DVD. I had a few DVDs of the recordings, but sadly, I have lost them."

"I had lost contact with him," Joseph continued. "It was when you brought up the idea of the film project that I set about trying to trace him. Happily, I have located him in his film studio in Tema. He told me he is still in the film production business, and I would highly recommend him to you."

I asked Joseph to organize a Zoom meeting to get to know him better and to see how he interacts with the rest of the team. Eventually, a group Zoom meeting was held involving Joseph, Confidence, Mania, Richard, and myself.

He had no firm engagements then, so he happily agreed to join the team. We were all delighted and relieved to have found the right person for the job.

Affectionately known as Godfidence by his associates, Confidence did an excellent job.

Ultimately, the Ghana segment of the film was expanded, taking up approximately 90% of the total screen time.

Recognizing Godfidence's significant role in this expansion, he has rightly been designated as the principal director of the whole production.

As we approach the release, the reception of the film by the public remains uncertain. Whether the audience's response is favourable or unfavourable, one thing is certain: this project would not have reached a successful conclusion without Godfidence's unwavering dedication, hard work, and attention to detail.

***

As already stated, Joseph was responsible for organizing the Ghana auditions.

It is unnecessary to state here that, in a social media age, it was not difficult for me to follow developments in Ghana from the faraway UK.

He held two events—one in Accra and the other in Kumasi. Ghana's second largest city.

I mentioned earlier that I was surprised by the response when I placed notices on Backstage looking for actors in the UK.

The response to Joseph's adverts looking for actors was even more overwhelming.

In a developing country like Ghana, where youth unemployment is a pressing concern, one can imagine the applicants' eagerness to find engagement opportunities; it was indeed palpable.

I mentioned I found it difficult to turn down those who applied for roles in the UK.

Joseph was placed in a less enviable situation, for, as he told me, the applicants literally begged him to assign them roles. At any rate, the applicants' zeal to be part of the cast put us in a dilemma. Ultimately, we decided not to reject them; instead, we kept everyone on board, hoping to find roles for them as supporting artists.

**

Assembling Crew and Equipment

How do I find the crew and equipment for the production in Ghana? I wondered. Having been away from Ghana for a while, I was unfamiliar with the local film scene. Everyone was talking about Nollywood, the well-established film industry in Nigeria, which made me curious about the situation in Ghana.

Upon my return, I was pleasantly surprised to discover that while Ghana's film industry may not yet rival Nigeria's Nollywood, it shows promising growth and development.

Ghana has companies that rent out equipment, agencies for booking actors, and agencies involved in location hire, making the production process more manageable.

Except for the camera, which I decided to purchase for my production, we could easily source all the necessary equipment from local rental companies.

Godfidence was pivotal in guiding us toward the right crew and suitable rental companies for our equipment needs.

With his extensive experience in the Ghanaian film industry, he has a network of contacts throughout the industry, particularly in and around the capital, Accra.

**

The filming segment in Ghana was divided into two main locations: Mpintimpi, my birth village, and Accra, the capital city. Approximately 80% of the filming took place in Mpintimpi, while the remaining 20% was filmed in Accra. I won't go into detail about the extensive planning the Ghana team conducted ahead of the filming sessions, as I'd rather not bore my readers.

**

I previously mentioned that I reckoned with the comparatively lower wages and equipment hire costs in Ghana to help us complete the project despite our limited budget.

Even so, we would have faced significant financial challenges if we had conducted most of the filming in the capital, Accra, or any other major town in the country.

Indeed, with all my optimism, I doubt if the Legacy Africa film project would have been realized financially had it not been for the significant cost-saving benefits I derived from filming at Mpintimpi and the two nearby towns of Nyafoman and Akuase.

The entire team, which included the director, cast, crew, and ancillary staff, comprised over 50 individuals. Each of us spent an average of ten days in the village. With my limited resources, how could I have managed to house and feed the entire team for a ten-day period in Accra?

Fortunately, the favorable conditions in Mpintimpi, my birthplace, allowed us to complete the project with minimal resources.

**

Mpintimpi is located approximately 120 kilometers northwest of Accra. To reach the village from Accra, take the main road toward Kumasi. At Nkawkaw, about 100 kilometers north of Accra, exit the main road and turn left onto the road leading to New Abirem. Mpintimpi is situated along the Nkawkaw-New Abirem road, roughly thirty kilometers from Nkawkaw. The journey from Accra to Mpintimpi typically takes 3 to 4 hours, depending on traffic conditions.

Previously, the road to Mpintimpi was known for its rugged terrain and potholes, which often caused inconvenience. However, it is a relief to announce that the road has undergone significant repairs and is now paved, ensuring a smoother and more accessible journey.

For most of our team, who were coming from Accra and its surrounding areas, we arranged a minibus to ensure a comfortable trip with all the filming equipment. The remaining team members from various parts of the country, including Kumasi, made their own transportation arrangements.

**

When I was growing up in my small village, we had no electricity, tap water, or modern sewage systems. More than half a century later, the community has made steady progress in amenity provision.

In terms of electricity, the village is now connected to the national grid. However, given the low incomes of the residents, one might wonder if everyone can afford their electricity bills. From what I understand, most people only turn on the lights for a few hours each night to manage their expenses.

When it comes to water, during my childhood in the village, our main water supply came from the Nwi River, which is a kilometer away. We also had access to a single well dug by the community, located not far from our home, which served the entire village. Unfortunately, the well's water supply was often unreliable and would frequently run dry during the dry season.

I almost forgot to mention the rainwater we collected in large steel containers from the drains positioned at the edges of our corrugated roofing.

Fortunately, the water supply situation has improved today, thanks to borehole technology, which allows for drilling deep into the earth to access generally good-quality water from significant depths below the surface.

When I was growing up, the village had two pit latrines serving the male and female populations, respectively. However, the town has made significant strides in this area. Now, a number of modern toilets can be accessed in the village.

The introduction of electricity in the village has sparked a wave of entrepreneurial spirit. Several individuals have set up shops, offering a variety of chilled drinks—water, soft drinks, beer, etc.—to those who can afford them.

Thus, compared to the conditions prevailing when I was growing up several years before, the village was relatively well-placed to host the filming team.

**

How could the Production provide accommodation for approximately 50 individuals in my small hometown? Although the settlement has grown significantly since my childhood, it can still be described as a small town, and there wasn't enough sleeping rooms to host the entire group.

Recognizing the limitations of Mpintimpi, Joseph explored nearby towns that could provide suitable accommodation for the filming crew. Afosu and New Abirem, located about five and seven kilometers to the south of our settlement, emerged as viable options.

Both Afosu and New Abirem boasted hotels and guesthouses of commendable quality. While the daily rates at these facilities were lower than those in larger cities like Accra and Kumasi, the overall cost of accommodating around 50 individuals for the ten days we planned to film would still be significant.

After a thorough discussion with Joseph, a familiar face in the village, we decided to leverage our local connections to secure accommodation for a portion of the crew, supporting artists, and non-essential staff. The more prominent members—such as the Executive Producer, the Director, Joseph, and a few senior cast members—would be accommodated in hotels.

**

I am deeply grateful to my daughter Ama, the first child of my late brother Emmanuel. Readers should recall what I said earlier regarding our Akan culture. So, Amma is not my niece but my most senior daughter, the first grandchild of my late parents.

She played a crucial role in helping us resolve our accommodation problem.

Through her diligence and handwork, she has built a decent residence in the village. Hers is indeed the most prominent building in the little settlement boasting several rooms..

Initially, we contacted her to discuss renting a couple of the rooms for the group.

"No, how can I rent them out to my Papa?"

"No, Ama, the filming is a business venture, so you should not be disadvantaged", I stated

"No, I won't charge my Papa anything. I don't charge outsiders who come to lodge with me; how can I charge you?"

"What do you mean by outsiders?" I inquired.

"You know what, Papa?" She began." Whenever there is a funeral here, people come to beg for me to house their relatives who are arriving from outside. They all expect me to place the rooms at their disposal free of charge!"

"No, Ama, you cannot do that. You will go bankrupt. At least they will have to pay your electricity bills." I advised her.

"The moment I ask them to pay, they will accuse me of being cold-hearted!"

"No, no; that cannot go on. You are ruining your finances!"

"I tell you what; on not a few occasions, my guests have left me with a blocked WC. I usually place toilet rolls at their disposal. When it gets exhausted, instead of going to the shops to acquire some, they resort to stiff paper and hard tissue, which eventually lead to sewage blockage!"

At that juncture, I recalled an experience I made while visiting the village with the rest of my family in 2007. During our stay, I kept dishing out money to individuals who had contacted me with their diverse problems. Karen, my daughter, who was strange to the culture, told me in the face, "Papa, you are committing financial suicide!"

Ama found herself in a similar situation to mine—with a bit of a difference, I should say. In my case, it involved individuals who were in genuine financial need.

The situation here was different. The guests she was opening her home to at no cost were taking advantage of her. They had travelled to the village for funerals, so at least they had money to pay for their transportation. Therefore, they should be in a position to pay for the sleepover.

**

Knowing that Ama was resolute in refusing my payment offer, I chose not to prolong the discussion. I was determined not to exploit her and had a plan in mind that I would put into action at the end of our stay.

Turning to her, I stated:

"You just do what you can for us; I will ensure you are not disadvantaged."

"I can place three rooms at your disposal."

"Thanks for your kind gesture. Since we plan to accommodate a minimum of two individuals in a room, it would imply accommodating at least half a dozen of the team." Ama's generosity was evident, and I couldn't help but feel appreciative of her willingness to help.

Just as I was about to leave my daughter Ama to attend to something else, she turned to me and began.

"Papa, do you see the storey building at the other end of the compound?"

"Yes, is it your property?"

"Not exactly. It belongs to your grandson Frank, my third child. He is not around—I am the caretaker. The building boasts a large hall. If your visitors would not mind sleeping on mattresses spread on the floor, it could accommodate a good twenty of them!"

"That's a great idea, Ama," I said. "I don'tt expect any member of the team to object to sleeping on mattresses spread out on the floor. After all, we are not here for a luxury holiday; we are here to work. My only concern is finding enough mattresses for everyone."

At that point, Ama turned to Joseph, who was attentively following the conversation. "Joseph, as you know, a resident of the village has made it her business to rent out mattresses to outsiders who visit the village, usually for funerals of their relatives. I suggest you check with her to see how many mattresses she has available."

Joseph quickly left to get in touch with her, and fortunately, she had twenty mattresses available. We decided to rent all of them. As expected, the dealer was thrilled at the opportunity to rent a significant number of mattresses for an extended period.

On our part, we were delighted to have found an affordable solution to our accommodation needs.

In the end, Ama—bless her—provided accommodation for more than two dozen team members.

About a dozen remaining group members were hosted in various homes of extended family members, friends, and old associates. The remainder of the group, about ten in number, along with Joseph, the director, and me, stayed at a hotel in New Abirem.

At the end of our stay, I handed Joseph an envelope containing a decent sum, the exact amount of which I prefer not to reveal, to present to Ama.

Later, I learned she was utterly shocked when she realized the amount inside the envelope. "This will cover my electricity and water bills for the entire year and beyond!" she exclaimed at the top of her voice.

Ama's kindness had already saved us a considerable sum, but the unexpected nature of my donation took her by surprise. It was a moment filled with gratitude and joy, a beautiful exchange that left us both feeling the warmth of generosity.

**

Long before we left for the village, Joseph began making preparations for the team's boarding needs. Based on his advice, we decided to hire some women from the small settlement to provide meals for the team. We entrusted my sister Manu, who is six years younger than me, with organizing the group of women.

To achieve this, we meticulously planned and purchased a good stock of ingredients needed to prepare various popular Ghanaian dishes. The plan was to offer two meals daily featuring traditional dishes such as fufu, banku, and ampesi.

Initially, the group responded positively to the locally prepared meals. However, as our stay continued, some members started to complain about the lack of variety in the meals. "We thought we would have more delicious options, like jollof rice, egg fried rice, fried chicken, and chips, ordered from a restaurant!" the majority grumbled.

To boost morale, I decided to address their request for more variety by ordering meals from a restaurant in one of the neighboring towns during the last few days of the filming session.

**

Before I report on the actual filming, I want to address some challenges we encountered that were not specific to Mpintipmi but of general nature.

"DUMSOR, DUMSOR"

We faced a challenge that filmmakers in developed countries are unlikely to encounter: frequent power outages. Ghana has been experiencing persistent and erratic power outages for an extended period, leading the local population to coin the term "Dumsor" to describe this situation.

This term literally means "lights off—lights on." Although authorities have attempted to address the issue over the years, it remains a significant problem.

As we prepared for the shoot in the village, our team emphasized the issue of power outages. I suggested renting a suitable generator as a backup. I was assured that this arrangement had been made. However, upon arriving in the village, we discovered that we had traveled without a backup generator!

Just after we completed our preparations and began filming on the first day, "dumsor; dumsor" struck unexpectedly. This sudden power outage disrupted our filming schedule, resulting in several hours of delay and affecting our momentum. Unfortunately, the same issue occurred again the following day.

"No, this cannot continue; otherwise, we will end up spending several more days here," the Director said, frustration clearly visible on his face.

"How can we get a generator in this remote village?" another team member wondered.

"I know where we can rent one!" Douglas suggested. He was a resident of the village and a good friend of mine; our friendship began during our boyhood and had lasted over the years. He had been with the team since our arrival in the village.

"Where?" I asked.

"At Afosu," he replied. (Afosu is a larger settlement about five kilometers south of Mpintimpi.)

"If you can provide the funds, I will quickly head there and rent one."

"Okay, please go ahead," I replied.

About three hours later, he returned with a generator.

However, our excitement over obtaining the generator was short-lived. Its capacity was insufficient; while it could power the lights, it could not support the camera and other filming equipment.

Ultimately, we had to rely on the national electricity grid, which proved to be unreliable throughout our filming, causing significant delays in our schedule.

I don't know what the future holds, but if I need to make another film in the country, acquiring a silent generator with adequate capacity will be my top priority.

**

Climate Change Uncertainties

There is a lot of discussion these days about climate change. While some people believe it is real, others dismiss it as "fake news." I don't intend to debate this topic in this presentation.

However, I have noticed unexpected changes in the climate of Mpintimpi. When I lived there several years ago, it

rarely rained in October. On the few occasions when it did
rain, it usually occurred in the evening or at night, and it
lasted only a short time. Although my awareness of the typically dry October weather didn't influence my decision to
film there during that month, I thought the generally good
weather would work to our advantage. In other words, I
expected favorable weather without rain interruptions
during our filming sessions. One can therefore imagine my
sheer astonishment when the skies opened up in a torrential
downpour around midday the day after our arrival!

"What's happening with our weather?" I blurted out,
my frustration evident as I turned to Bempong my close
relative.

"Well, things have changed," he replied, his voice tinged
with concern. "As you know, in the past, we expected the
rainy season to occur between May and July. But now, we
are in mid-October, and it feels like we are in the middle of
the rainy season."

"This just isn't right!" I exclaimed, struggling to com-
prehend the abnormality of the situation.

"Well, my dear, the weather has become unpredictable. In the past, we knew when the rains would arrive.
We planted our crops with the expectation of rain and were
rarely disappointed. But now, that pattern seems almost
broken, and we all feel the impact."

Climate change was indeed affecting Ghana. In my
online research, I discovered that it was not only the residents of Mpintimpi who were concerned; the entire farming
community of the country was expressing similar worries.

Just two days before the filming was scheduled to begin, it rained for most of the day. As the rain poured down relentlessly, I looked to the heavens and prayed for favorable weather during our shoot.

I was fortunate that my prayers were answered: the weather was perfect throughout the ten-day filming period. On the rare occasions when it rained, it was either early in the morning, stopping before we began filming, or late in the evening after we had completed or were nearing the end of our filming session for the day.

**

Before delving into our filming experience in Mpintimpi, I want to highlight an important cultural nuance.

In certain parts of the world, particularly in the West, elected mayors typically govern communities. However, in my native Ghana, each community is led by a traditional leader or chief. This leadership role is inherited and carries significant responsibilities.

Tradition dictates that when someone wishes to organize an event, such as our planned filming in the community, they must notify the chief and seek his approval. While this is generally a formality, it is crucial to follow the procedure. Failing to do so may lead to social sanctions, which could include a monetary fine or a request to donate a few bottles of alcoholic drinks—or both—to the chief. The chief does not keep everything for himself but shares with his subchiefs and other traditional leaders.

Aware of this social norm, Joseph and a few team members who visited the village several weeks ahead of the filming schedule to undertake the location scouting did indeed call on the chief to inform him about our plans.

However, that initial notification was not sufficient. We were expected to inform him again upon our arrival to notify him about the actual filming. Unfortunately, due to our busy schedule, we overlooked this detail.

My sister, Manu, continually reminded me of this oversight and emphasized the need to rectify the situation as soon as possible.

Finally, on the third day, I called on the most revered member of the community. He welcomed me warmly to his residence. He is not a stranger to me. I am several years older than him and have known him since he was a young boy, although his position as a traditional leader now places him above me in the community.

If he was displeased with my failure to adhere to tradition, he didn't show it. Instead, our conversation was light-hearted and filled with laughter as we reminisced about our shared experiences growing up in our small village, evoking a strong sense of nostalgia.

**

Much of the filming in Mpintimpi focused on recreating my birth and early years spent there. Although the humble two-room mud house I grew up in still exists, it is now uninhabited. After our parents passed away several years ago, my sister Manu initially lived in that house. However, she has since built a small dwelling about two hundred meters away.

The Production had the option to restore the old house to its original condition, but due to our limited time, we decided against that approach. Instead, we opted to find alternative locations that resembled the original setting. As mentioned earlier, the team visited the village several days before filming to scout potential locations.

After exploring various sites in and around the small settlement, we eventually selected an area that resembled my family home.

However, this site had one drawback: it belonged to a family that had decided to build their residence about three hundred metres outside the village boundaries. One might wonder why they chose to live away from the settlement. The reason is that they wanted to be close to their cocoa farm, allowing them to avoid the daily walk to work.

There was a slight issue with this location. As already stated it was isolated from the village and could only be accessed by a narrow bush path. To reach it, one also had to cross a makeshift wooden bridge over a river. The narrowness of the path and the poor condition of the bridge made it impossible for us to drive our vehicles there. What should we do?

With a firm resolve to utilize that location despite the challenges we faced, the team began a dialogue with a group of young, energetic men from the settlement. We asked if some of them would be willing to carry our equipment and other filming materials on their heads and shoulders to the site for a negotiated fee. While this may seem unusual to those unfamiliar with our surroundings, it is actually a quite common practice in our society. The services of head porters are frequently employed in various parts of the country, particularly in cities and large towns.

After diligent efforts, we found about half a dozen individuals who promised to carry on the assignment for an agreed fee.

On the day of filming, we set out to find the individuals who had promised to serve as our head porters, but to our disappointment, none of them showed up. We soon discovered that the owner of a makeshift gold mining site about half a kilometer from the settlement had offered them higher wages to work for him that day.

We had fallen victim to "Galamansay," which refers to illegal makeshift gold mining in Ghana. As I write this, it remains a significant issue in the country. Driven by the hope of making quick money, many individuals are involved in the practice. Unfortunately, it has resulted in substantial pollution of water bodies nationwide. Although various governments have attempted to address the problem, it still persists.

**

The day of filming had arrived. It was already past 8 a.m. The Director had planned to begin filming the circumstances of my birth around 10 am.

The clock was ticking, and the Director's plan was at a standstill. What was to be done?

At that juncture, Douglas the friend from my boyhood days I referred to above turned to me and began:

"Come with me. I will speak to a family or two whose dwellings resemble where you grew up. "

"Who?" I inquired.

"Well, they moved into the settlement about two decades ago—long after you have left."

It was a stark realization. Despite my regular visits, the place I once called home had changed. Several new residents had moved into the settlement whom I did not know. As it were, I had become a stranger in my backyard. But this was not the time for introspection. We needed a solution, and we needed it fast!

The team followed Douglas in our urgent quest to find a last-minute solution. In the village, no fences separate homes, allowing anyone to enter another person's house without prior notice. Notwithstanding, the lady of the first home we visited was taken aback by the sudden arrival of about half a dozen strangers, in addition to Douglas.

To ease her anxiety, Douglas quickly began explaining the reason for our visit. He introduced me, emphasizing my connection to the village, the purpose of our stay in the village, and the desperate situation we were in. Before she could respond, her husband, who had gone to the nearby woods to fetch something, returned home. After a brief consultation, the pair kindly agreed to our request to film at their modest home.

Permitting us to film in their humble residence would cause considerable discomfort to the family. It was a two-room mud house. It was a type of chamber and hall arrangement. The children slept in the small hall whilst the parents used the other room as their chamber. One had to pass through the hall to reach the sleeping room.

We did most of the filming in the hall. There were indeed times when filming proceeded too late in the night, leading them to hang around on the open compound until the session was over before retiring to bed.

Recognizing their sacrifice, I generously compensated them with a reasonable sum. When I handed them the money I had set aside for them, they were visibly moved, and for a moment, words seemed to escape them.

What I considered a modest compensation was, in reality, a significant lifeline for them.

It is a hand-to-mouth existence in the community. The average resident in the village counts themselves blessed when they earn enough to get through the day—saving even a few cedis in a day is a dream to most residents.

I undeniably benefited from their kind gesture, for which I am eternally grateful.

**

Part of the storyline revolves around a local Member of Parliament (MP) who failed to fulfill his promises to provide various facilities for his constituency, contrary to what he had pledged during his election campaign. The clinic in the area, neglected by the ruling party he represented, lacked basic equipment and essential supplies. The irony was stark when the MP, who had not provided for the clinic, was rushed to this very poorly equipped facility after suffering a cardiac arrest during a campaign tour.

We needed to find a suitable location to film this scene. In my childhood, the only hospital serving our village and its surroundings was located in Nkawkaw, about 30 kilometers away. Meanwhile, a health post had been established in Akuase, roughly seven kilometers north of Mpintimpi.

We decided to approach the authorities of the clinic to request permission to film on their premises. To our surprise, they not only granted our request but also offered the facility to us free of charge.

Additionally, it's important to note that, as with all our filming locations in Ghana, we were not required to present public liability insurance coverage before being permitted to use the site.

**

The primary school where I began my academic journey was not left out in my first venture into film production. The film indeed displays scenes from my early school days. A production team with a big wallet could have created a similar scene at a different location. It is superfluous to mention here that was not the case with us. So we explored the possibility of filming in the same locality.

My academic journey began at the Nyafoman Roman Catholic Primary School, two miles north of Mpintimpi. The original school building, a humble structure, has been graced with a more substantial, modern building constructed nearby. The old school building, a resilient symbol of time's passage, still stands, albeit in a state of disrepair, a poignant contrast to the vibrant memories it holds.

Gratefully, the local authority, which still manages the property, generously granted us free access to the old building for our filming.

As I stepped back into the now dilapidated rooms of my Primary school, my mind was flooded with memories of the days when I, the little schoolboy so short in stature that I gained the acronym "Mpintipim dwarf," took my seat in the humble environs and began the academic journey. How could I, the poor pupil whose parents hardly earned a couple hundred dollars in annual income, then imagine I would make it to medical school in Germany?

Furthermore, the idea that I would return to the school one day to film scenes from my humble academic beginnings as part of a film meant to inspire the youth of Africa to work hard to uplift the fortunes of the continent was something far, far beyond what I could ever imagine.

**

After ten days of filming, we finally completed our sessions in Mpintimpi and bid farewell to the small village.

Leaving my birthplace filled me with mixed emotions—both joy and sadness.

Despite the challenges we faced during filming, I was pleased we captured all the scenes related to the settlement. The children of the settlement especially enjoyed the visitors in their village. Based on their expressions, they were utterly captivated by our filming equipment and the overall experience. Their innocent curiosity added a delightful charm to our time there.

I shared my feelings of sadness with the village residents. Our presence had brought some vibrancy to the community and boosted economic activity, benefiting several shops that sold water, soft drinks, and ready-made food.

One could see the sadness on their faces as we said goodbye and headed back to where we had come from.

The journey back to Accra was uneventful.

**

We needed to film various scenes on the streets of Accra. After being away for some time, I was unfamiliar with the laws regulating public filming in the city, so I turned to our production manager for clarification.

"We can go ahead without seeking permission," he informed me.

"Aren't we going to get into trouble?" I asked.

"We've filmed scenes on the street without any issues before, so I don't think we will have any problems this time," he assured me.

He was right; no one confronted us about needing a permit during our filming sessions. I found it intriguing how the informal nature of street filming in Accra contrasted with the strict regulations we faced in London. As already reported, in London, we had to provide a Public Liability Insurance certificate before our application to film in a park could even be considered, and there were additional charges for using the space.

Among the scenes we filmed on the streets of Accra were interviews with passersby, where we asked about their views on the economy and their expectations on the government to improve their situation.

As expected, the unique experience of filming on the streets attracted the curiosity of onlookers, adding an authentic touch to our project.

"What is going on here?" many pedestrians queried. As time allowed, we provided them with a brief explanation of our project and emphasized the crucial role they play in building anticipation for our film's upcoming release. It was a fantastic opportunity to engage with potential viewers and make them feel valued.

**

One of the highlights of our filming journey in Ghana was capturing the grand outdoor ceremony celebrating the newly completed mansion of the Member of Parliament (MP) representing the constituency where Mpintimpi is located.

Perched atop a gently sloping hill in an affluent area of the Ghanaian capital, the magnificent mansion commands attention with its timeless elegance and grandeur.

You might wonder why an MP from a remote area, far removed from Accra, would choose to build a mansion so distant from his own constituency.

While the film is a work of fiction, it mirrors real-life situations. Accra has become a magnet for many people in the country, making it quite common for MPs from distant regions to invest in property in the capital.

The ceremony was a vibrant display of pomp and affluence, with distinguished guests filling the halls of the luxurious home. The lively, rhythmic beats of African music filled the air, adding to the energetic atmosphere. Guests adorned in a kaleidoscope of colorful African costumes truly brought to life the rich tapestry of Ghanaian culture and tradition.

As I admired the vibrant spectacle before me, I couldn't help but wonder if the bright sun influences the general love Africans have for color.

Does the ever-present sunny sky truly inspire our passion for vibrant hues? I can only wonder.

Chapter 4

Post-Production, Marketing & Miscellaneous

I previously shared that I learned about the stages of film production from the internet. The development stage occurs before pre-production, and production follows the pre-production steps. After much effort, we completed the first three stages, and it was now time to move into the post-production stage.

As we were about to wrap up the filming activities, Godfidence, the director, asked me, "Boss, are you ready to begin the post-production journey, or would you prefer to pause and start it later?"

"Of course, let's proceed. I've already invested significant money and want to ensure that I can recoup my investment." I replied,

"I understand the financial sacrifice you've made. Since you've mentioned that your finances are stretched,

I just wanted to confirm if you have enough funds for the post-production work." He responded.

"So, how much are we looking at regarding funds?" I asked.

"It's quite substantial; it could be between twenty and thirty per cent of what you have spent so far on production if not more!" He answered.

"Really?" I queried. My surprise at the potential cost of post-production became evident as the financial burden began to sink in.

He then sat me down and provided a detailed briefing on the post-production process, the outline of which I now share with the reader.

1. Storage: The first step is to store the footage on one or more hard drives securely.
2. Editing: At this stage, the footage is edited for continuity, pacing, and overall storytelling.
3. Audio: Sound editors assemble the audio, removing unwanted noises and adding sound effects. If any dialogue is unclear, the actors are invited back to the studio for automated dialogue replacement, which is then integrated into the film's audio track.
4. Music: The music supervisor manages the musical elements, acquiring original music or securing publishing rights for copyrighted songs.
5. Mixing: The sound mixer layers the audio, dialogue, and music, adjusting and enhancing sounds as necessary.

6. Visual Effects: Visual effects, including computer-generated imagery, are added to enhance the film.
7. Colour Grading: The colourist undertakes colour grading to ensure the visuals have the desired look and feel.
8. Graphics: Editors create graphics, title cards, and opening and closing credits and integrate them into the film.
9. Trailer Creation: Once the movie has been thoroughly edited and polished, a separate editing team develops a compelling trailer designed to attract audiences.

**

The director's assessment of the post-production costs was spot on, with the costs incurred in this phase amounting to approximately a third of the total project expenditure.

Post-production is not only expensive but also time-consuming. While the filming took only a few weeks, the post-production phase required several months of hard work from the director and his dedicated editing team.

**

In every life situation, we all encounter unexpected twists and turns. It's a shared part of our human experience.

As a novice in film production, I've realised that film-making's collaborative nature amplifies the impact of life's unexpected twists. Indeed, the diverse roles of individuals in a film set mean that any unforeseen event could disrupt the entire process.

Just an example: Assuming every crew department—camera, light, sound, makeup etc—is ready to shoot on a particular day, and the lead actor suddenly falls ill!

An unexpected event can disrupt the shooting schedule and create a financial burden. The costs associated with rescheduling, rebooking locations, and paying the crew for additional days can significantly impact the budget.

For productions with large budgets, these additional costs can often be absorbed due to their financial reserves and the ability to secure extra funding. However, for a film producer like me, working with a minimal budget, any unexpected expenses can have a substantial effect on the overall production.

Thankfully, we did not have to postpone or cancel a filming set due to diseases. As mentioned, power outages and weather issues caused delays on a few filming days, but cancelling the whole day's schedule due to the above factors did not happen to us.

In light of the above, I breathed a sigh of relief when my director declared the end of the filming sessions and announced the beginning of the post-production stage—a bit premature, as it turned out.

**

As previously mentioned, the production in London was directed by a different individual. The person responsible for producing the Ghana segment eventually took on the role of overall director for the entire film. Due to his busy schedule managing the Ghana production, he initially only had the chance to briefly review the London footage to familiarize himself with what had already been filmed.

During the post-production phase, as he began editing the London footage, he noticed gaps in the storyline that he believed needed to be addressed to achieve the best possible outcome. At the start of January 2025, during our weekly Zoom meeting, he brought up the issue:

"I aim to produce a high-quality film. However, I have identified interruptions in the storyline. We need to film these gaps, so you must come down to Ghana," he stated.

I agreed and traveled to Ghana as requested. After a few days of filming, the work was completed, and I returned to the UK.

**

At the beginning of March, as we were starting to plan the release of the film, we had our usual weekly Zoom meeting. The Director, whose attention to detail I have come to admire, opened the meeting in a way I least expected:

"You may not like what you're about to hear. To ensure a perfect production, we need to film an additional scene that involves you!"

"Could you please repeat that?"I replied, pretending not to have fully understood him.

"Sure," he responded. "We are not striving for a film of meager quality. On the contrary, we aim for a high-quality movie that has a chance of being accepted by leading platforms like Netflix. To achieve this, we must add an additional scene involving you. We need to do this for the sake of audience satisfaction; otherwise, they will be left with unanswered questions."

"Well, if you believe we need the additional scene, please go ahead and organize it," I replied.

"To stick to our production schedule, we must complete this in the next few days," he added.

"Okay, I will book a flight as soon as we finish the meeting."

With that, I prepared for my third trip to Ghana for the production.

On the eve of my flight, while I was in the process of packing, Rita turned to me and said, "Let's hope this is the last time the team needs you in Ghana."

"I hope so too!" I replied.

**

"Third time lucky!" is a well-known saying, and for me, it turned out to be true.

After traveling to Ghana for the third time to work on the Legacy Africa project, I returned to the UK hoping it would be the last time my Director would need me to film additional scenes for the project.

Fortunately, my hope was fulfilled. Not long after I returned to the UK, the Director called to inform me that he was not only satisfied with our footage but also very impressed. He stated that no further filming was necessary.

However, this didn't mean that was the last time I would encounter unexpected post-production costs associated with the project. While in the final stages of editing and preparing to submit the work to the Ghana Film Authorities for rating, the Director sent a WhatsApp message announcing an unexpected setback.

This setback threatened to delay the project's already tight timeline. Earlier, I had mentioned the frequent electricity outages that have earned the term "dumsor." The Director informed me that on one particular day, while he was busy colour-grading the project, there was a power outage. It took some time for the power to be restored, and when he turned on the monitor in hopes of continuing his work, he discovered it had completely stopped functioning.

He urgently needed a replacement, and time was of the essence. I encouraged him to look for a monitor in the local market, but he informed me that the required high-quality monitor was unavailable in Ghana. Ultimately, I had to purchase the specified monitor in the UK. Given the urgency, I opted to ship it by air instead of sea freight, which resulted in substantial shipping costs.

**

I have invested a significant amount of time, energy, and money into the Legacy Africa film project, and it is now time to market it. Even before the project reached the post-production stage, I diligently researched effective marketing strategies online, which I plan to pursue.

I have heard stories of other films that required substantial investments but did not yield expected returns. I am fully aware of the risks involved in the film industry and can only hope and pray I will be spared a similar fate; yes, that I can at least retrieve the investment poured into it.

**

Roll call of a Segment of the Production Team

Before concluding my narration, I want to briefly profile a section of the production team.

As previously mentioned, the production team of a film involves a wide range of creative and logistical roles that are essential for bringing a film from concept to screen.

Space will not permit me to profile every one of them engaged in the production of Legacy Africa.

I hope those who are not included here will not feel disappointed. Please know that your contributions to the project's successful completion are highly valued and appreciated. Yes indeed, the critical role played by each team member is recognized and respected.

Dr ROBERT PEPRAH-GYAMFI

With a diverse background as a medical doctor, author, evangelist, and film producer, he also takes on the leading role in the film. His only acting experience was during his secondary school years at his alma mater, Oda Secondary School, from 1971 to 1976. As a member of the Dramatic Society, he was assigned various roles in plays performed by the club to entertain the entire school. Could these early experiences have been a way for Providence to prepare him for the role he now plays in this film?

CONFIDENCE LOSU

Confidence, a filmmaker known for his unique approach to the industry, is committed to excellence in all his works. His portfolio includes critically acclaimed works such as "War from the Archives" (2021), "Zoli" (2018), and "Heaven's Amen" (2017). His transformative abilities and attention to detail have enabled him to turn the LEGACY AFRICA screenplay into a vibrant and captivating masterpiece.

MUKHTAR AZEEZ

Muktar, in his own words: As a motivated young person, I find joy in the art of make-believe. My time in the local drama society has allowed me to learn and adapt to diverse acting and stage performance skills. I am open to a wide range of acting, advertising, and modelling opportunities across England and beyond and ready to bring my adaptability to any role, local or international.

VYRETTA DADSON

A vibrant teenage girl, she infused enthusiasm into her role as Bola, a young Nigerian schoolgirl. Together with Kwasi, she engaged the elderly Kofi in a thoughtful conversation about tackling some of the challenges facing the African continent.

BRIGITTE MILLAR

Brigitte is an award-winning actress with a wealth of experience from her diverse roles in various films. Notable
appearances include the James Bond films *Spectre* and
No Time to Die, as well as an adaptation of *Harry Potter
and the Order of the Phoenix*. Her outstanding portrayal
of Professor Schmidt, the anatomy professor at Hannover
Medical School, showcases the excellence that comes from
her extensive acting career.

GEMMA SCHITO

Gemma, driven by her unwavering passion for acting and singing, took on the unenviable role of one of Kwasi's four classmates who bullied him because of his African heritage. Her dedication to her craft is evident as she excels in transforming herself to portray various characters. Even when faced with negative feedback, she perseveres, bringing her commitment and talent to the difficult task of playing Kwasi's bully.

RICHARD CUNNINGHAM

Richard played a vital and multifaceted role similar to that of a Production Manager for the London filming. His responsibilities included organizing auditions, managing administrative tasks, securing filming locations, and coordinating logistics to ensure the smooth operation of the production.

JOSEPH BAAFI GYAMFI

Joseph is a dynamic young man brimming with energy. He took an active role in all aspects of organizing the Ghana production. This included overseeing administrative tasks, securing filming locations and coordinating logistics to ensuring the smooth running of the production.

**

I have done my duty!

I sincerely hope that LEGACY AFRICA does not fade into obscurity but instead gains substantial viewership, allowing me to recoup my investment. The success of the film is not just a personal goal; it is a crucial step toward achieving Legacy Africa's long-term vision of inspiring and igniting transformation in Africa, particularly among the continent's youth, who hold the key to a brighter future.

I genuinely wish that both current and future leaders of Africa would understand the message the film seeks to convey: a call for good governance and a rejection of vices such as corruption, misappropriation of public funds, fraud etc.

I hope that the film not only instills a spirit of integrity and accountability but also serves as a powerful catalyst for positive change in the fortunes of the Sunshine Continent.

If a significant number of viewers in Africa, especially the youth—the leaders of tomorrow—embrace the noble virtues of honesty, accountability, and a sense of duty in their public lives, I would consider my mission accomplished.